Buddhism & The Enneagram

Second Edition

Mary R. Bast, Ph.D.

Copyright © 2014 Mary R. Bast, Ph.D.
All rights reserved.

ISBN: 1502951525
ISBN-13: 978-1502951526

*There is a song inside, a voice ripe for expression,
but I am bound by the rules and remain in the shadow.*
(J. Albrecht, *Psychological Perspectives*, 1992)

CONTENTS

1	So Many Ways to Cope	1
2	Finding Your Unique Satori	3
3	The Gift of Patience (Ones)	7
4	The Journey to Loving-Kindness (Twos)	11
5	The Absolute Truth: Being vs. Doing (Threes)	13
6	Singing in Our Chains (Fours)	15
7	Holding the Spade in Our Empty Hands (Fives)	17
8	Swimming with the Dolphins (Sixes)	19
9	The Beauty and the Beast (Sevens)	21
10	Take Refuge in the Community (Eights)	25
11	Breathe In, Breathe Out (Nines)	27

SO MANY WAYS TO COPE

We have so many ways to cope with life, many ways to worship comfort and pleasantness. All are based on the same thing: the fear of encountering any kind of unpleasantness. Charlotte Joko Beck, "The Cocoon of Pain, *Nothing Special: Living Zen*

Paraphrased below is Joko Beck's summary of ways we avoid encountering life mindfully:

1. If we must have absolute order and control, have things our way and get angry if they're not, we think we can shut out our anxiety about death.

2. If we can please everyone, we imagine no unpleasantness will enter our life.

3. If we can be the star of the show – shining, wonderful, efficient – we hope to attract such an admiring audience we won't have to feel anything.

4. If we can withdraw from the world and entertain ourselves with our own fantasies and emotional upheavals, we think we can escape unpleasantness.

5. If we can be so smart we fit everything into some sort of plan or order, a complete intellectual understanding, then perhaps we won't be threatened.

6. If we can submit to an authority who tells us what to do, we don't have to carry responsibility for our lives or feel the anxiety of making a decision.

7. If we can pursue life madly, going after any pleasant sensation, perhaps we won't have to feel pain.

8. If we can tell others what to do, keep them well under control, under our foot, maybe they can't hurt us.

9. If we can *bliss out*, if we can be a mindless *buddha* relaxing in the sun, we don't have to assume any responsibility for the world's unpleasantness. We can just be happy.

In these many ways we worship "the god of no discomfort and no unpleasantness." We become lost in our "feverish efforts" and lose touch with the life that presents itself to us every moment.

Eventually these coping strategies cease to work because they're based on a perception of life we create, not on reality itself. When this happens, when our attempts to control life fail us, we're finally ready to "begin serious practice."

In "Enneagram Opportunities," Zen teacher Cheri Huber described a note posted at the Monastery:

> *We have many guidelines, but only one rule: We will use everything in our experience to see how we cause ourselves to suffer so we can drop it and end suffering.*

We're in good company, then, to consider the Enneagram's overlap with Buddhist teachings, as a way to notice specific coping strategies that hinder our attempts to be mindful.

In that spirit, I hope this small book will provide readers with new insights into the experience and spiritual paths of the nine Enneagram styles.

FINDING YOUR UNIQUE *SATORI*

The Enneagram offers powerful insights into our personality styles, but we sometimes forget it is primarily a vehicle for awakening.

The transformational journey is enhanced when we recognize both the self-fulfilling and self-defeating aspects of the illusory masks of *personality*. However, we remain asleep to the degree that we abide by our nine conditional rules of habit: "*I must...*

>*...correct what is wrong."*

>*...take care of others' needs."*

>*...achieve and get results."*

>*...regret what is missing in my life."*

>*...understand everything."*

>*...beware of potential problems/threats."*

>*...be positive, upbeat, look to the future."*

>*...be in control."*

>*...respond to others' ideas and expectations."*

While each of these nine coping strategies shows up in a primary *fixation* motivated by a *passion*, none of us is completely separate from the other eight. Ones, for example, are fixated on perfectionism (*I must correct what is wrong*) and their passion for anger. But who among us does not struggle with anger or have some perfectionistic behaviors? We each can benefit from the lessons of all nine.

I'm intrigued with the parallels between the Enneagram paths of transformation and the path of *satori* (liberation) in the Buddhist tradition. Both recommend:

- letting go of reliance on logic alone in the intuitive search for a new viewpoint;
- realizing the world is not as we've known it to be, because our ordinary knowing has been conditioned by life circumstances;
- releasing our habitual behaviors and beliefs and coming to know that everything is relative, conditioned, and impermanent.

Students of Buddhism in pursuit of *satori* are advised to cultivate the *paramitas* (perfections), considered essential to our progress as human beings. Some of these *paramitas* bear an uncanny resemblance to virtues associated with particular Enneagram styles.

I've relied on the translations of John Snelling in *The Buddhist Handbook* (with *Pali* equivalents, from the Theravada school):

adhitthana—determination
khanti—patience
metta—loving-kindness
sacca—truthfulness
upekkha—equanimity
dana—generosity
sila—morality
nekkhamma—renunciation
panna—wisdom
viriya—energy

In these pages I evoke the wisdom of Buddhism to inform our Enneagram paths. For example, the key noble quality of *adhitthana* (determination or commitment to spiritual practice) seems basic to all.

Following are nine additional parallels I've drawn:

1. Ones are impassioned by *anger* and fixated on *perfectionism*.

   Their path to *satori* is *khanti* or **patience**, the willingness to accept conditions that do not conform to one's ideal.

2. Twos have the passion of *pride* and are fixated on *entitlement* (caring for others is conditional).

   A path to *satori* is *metta* or **loving-kindness**, true compassion without expectation.

3. The passion of Threes is *vanity*, their fixation is *deception* (the need to see oneself and be seen as successful).

   Sacca or **truthfulness**—speaking from the essential self and not through personality needs—is a way to *satori*.

4. Fours live with the passion of *envy* and the fixation of *dissatisfaction*.

   Satori here can be sought through *upekkha* or **equanimity**; seeing all events as intrinsically neutral, knowing it's desire that grades things as "good" or "bad."

5. Fives have the passion of *hoarding*, with a fixation on *detachment* (desiring information but retreating from emotional connection).

   They can seek *satori* through *dana* or **generosity**, giving freely of oneself so energy flows outward.

6. For Sixes *fear* is the passion, *accusation* the fixation.

   Satori becomes possible with *sila* or **morality**; living with integrity, recognizing one's own contribution to situations instead of playing victim.

7. Sevens are driven by the passion of *gluttony*, with *enthusiasm* as a fixation.

   A path to *satori* is the well-known one of **renunciation**, seeking moderation and letting go of materialism.

8. The Eight fixation on *power and control* stems from the passion of *excess.*

   Wisdom is a way to *satori*; a shift to more altruistic and benign modes of operating, a focus on service to the world.

9. *Indolence* is the Nine's passion; the fixation is *self-forgetting* (resulting from their other-directedness).

   Energy is a way to *satori* for Nines; the willingness to stay focused on their own purpose, without distraction.

These Nine *paramitas* are explored more fully in the essays that follow.

THE GIFT OF PATIENCE

Tony Schwartz (*What Really Matters*) described each point on the Enneagram *as* "a defensive survival strategy that prompts a very narrow, habitual, and limited way of perceiving and responding to the world."

Each spiritual path can be seen as continually strengthening our connection with the universal and accurate discernment of our true purpose. But our survival strategies lead to distorted worldviews and attendant behaviors that impede such growth.

Being mindful of the nine Enneagram frames of reference increases our ability to observe how our fixations keep us from moving forward in spite of our best intentions.

Ones' passion of *anger*, for example, gives rise to *perfectionism*. Because their positive potential derives from their basic desire to be good, they try too hard to get things right. Open anger is relegated to the shadow except in circumstances where it feels totally justified—then anger shows up as a moral tirade.

My One client, Frank R., described his internal standards: "I'm not into this game of covering up things that aren't right. I've always tried to give people the benefit of the doubt, but I have a hard time when someone won't do the right thing."

According to one of his colleagues, "Frank is a big asset to the company and really wants to help, but he always thinks he's right, and that intolerance shows up no matter who he's talking to—if what they've done doesn't measure up to his standards he'll tell them, 'That's trash!'"

With coaching, Frank learned to deal more effectively with criticism (of self and others), to be more assertive (vs. aggressive), to give specific and descriptive feedback (vs. comments such as "That's trash!"), and to solve problems more creatively (instead of staying stuck in *either/or* thinking).

Most important, the practice of opening himself to other points of view also helped him grow in patience. He began to listen more closely when subordinates explained why they hadn't met a goal, and discovered his anger toward them had been masking his own fear of not being good enough.

As Frank became more able to embrace elements of himself he'd kept under control, he actually *felt* less angry, more patient. He didn't lower his standards, but his employees were more highly motivated by his listening and engaging them in problem-solving than they had been by his angry criticisms.

In the end, however, our ego traps are still engaged when we work only at the behavioral level, or even with attitudes and beliefs (e.g., "Well, I'm a One so I have to control my anger," or "I'm a Nine—self-forgetting—so I have to make sure my anger doesn't show up as passive aggression").

Our spiritual paths are not about control, but about letting go. When we're able to maintain a transformational focus, the passions and fixations are diminished, while the virtues are enhanced.

For those fixated on perfectionism this means instead of having to manage their anger, they become less angry and develop the gift of *patience*. How is this possible?

- As we study, reflect, discuss, seek understanding, and learn how we're programmed, we can recognize our fixations when they occur.

- As we embrace whatever shows up while maintaining an attitude of openness and non-attached equanimity, our passion is evoked in ways that shake the underpinnings of our patterns: we notice, without acting on destructive impulses.

- As we develop contemplative practices—breathing, relaxation, belly-centered meditation, and/or centering prayer—we begin to notice a centered attitude toward ongoing existence.

- As we offer appreciation when we experience ourselves without judgment, our obsolete responses drop away.

THE JOURNEY TO LOVING-KINDNESS

*One day you finally knew
what you had to do...
though the voices around you
kept shouting their bad advice...
"Mend my life!" ...*
(Mary Oliver, "The Journey")

All of us want love. And all of us, if we're honest, have at some time in our lives attached strings to our caring for someone else. This is a core dilemma for Enneagram Twos, particularly because they experience others wanting their lives mended, and that dependence can become too great a responsibility.

It's a paradox, of course, that Twos thrive on being needed and thus create the very dependency that burdens them. This is the passion of *pride*, the basis for their fixation of *entitlement*: feeling they're "owed" because of all they've given.

An unfortunate caricature is that Twos are solicitously, hand-wringingly, helpful people. I've only once run into someone this obvious (who punctuated every response with, "*Was that helpful?*").

So if you're a Two you may not recognize yourself in the caricature. You're likely, instead, to experience yourself as certain of your ability to cope with whatever is required; and as being needed to resolve difficult situations. Your pride may manifest as a genuine feeling of satisfaction that you were able to have an impact.

Let's say you've mentored someone who, because of your attention, has achieved a personal goal. As much as your efforts may have contributed to that achievement, pride is still a problem for you when your help has strings. If the person you've mentored, for example, decides to move in a different direction, how will you feel about all the effort you've expended? Will you feel let down? Even betrayed?

Twos create their own burdens because they find it so difficult to turn people down. One client observed, "My boss gets me to do things by saying, 'There's no one else here who can do it as well as you.'"

People of any Enneagram style may react to their discovery of such self-defeating characteristics by deciding they just won't "be that way" anymore. Wanting to change helps, but that alone won't make it happen.

These unconscious patterns are deeply embedded and largely unconscious. They can only be transformed through your ability to observe yourself honestly and without judgment.

The counter to pride is *humility*, not self-abasement or noisy humility, but accepting ourselves as we are, acknowledging our own limitations instead of focusing on the imperfections and neediness of those we care about and support.

The transformation will occur not by our doing anything, but by acknowledging and accepting these evidences of pride:

- Self-inflation.
- Believing we're entitled because we're so giving.
- Feeling offended when our efforts go unrecognized.
- Holding grudges over perceived betrayals.
- Viewing those we help as needy or lacking.
- Difficulty experiencing/acknowledging our own needs.

When we're no longer attached to pride, when we're able to offer support without strings, we're on the journey to true *loving-kindness*.

THE ABSOLUTE TRUTH: BEING VS. DOING

The word *persona*, which originally referred to ancient drama masks, was adopted by Carl Jung for the *masks* we wear, the roles we play as we adapt to external reality. As children developing a sense of self, we responded so completely to others' expectations our own *personas* became sources of self-deception. In our so-called *reality* we've come to believe we *are* the masks.

I discovered this quite profoundly for myself early in my consulting career as I experienced burn-out and—through fatigue with my work—realized how much vanity and self-deceit had driven me. I had gauged my success by extensive travel and designer suits, reveling in my value to clients, in being hired by "important" people.

One of my Three clients told me he had "a room full of empty trophies." Exactly.

The development path of *truthfulness*, then, refers to the enlightened ability to speak and act from the ways things really are and not through our personality needs.

When fixated on *self-deception* and driven by *vanity*, Threes need to see themselves and be seen by others as successful. This is consciously experienced as a drive toward achievement and results. I'm not a Three. Yet all of us manifest vanity. It may show up in the clothes we wear, in status-seeking, and competitiveness of all varieties—being the "best" athlete, having the "best" house, achieving the top organizational position, etc.

Threes are the least in touch with their feelings. My client, Sandy, was a workaholic dedicated to efficiency and results, no matter what the human cost. She was a loner who did not connect with her co-workers, focused only on accomplishments.

One day Sandy said to me, "You know how I am."

We had developed some trust by this point, so I told her the truth: "Actually, I don't. I suspect you tell me what you want me to think of you."

Sandy eventually learned to observe her compulsion to succeed and to talk about herself as a success, as well as her avoidance of failure. She noticed how often she told people what she thought they wanted to hear. She also saw how she failed to connect with others; instead of really listening she'd say, "Yes, we need to do that," when she'd already decided otherwise.

Even as she acknowledged these "failures," however, she began to kick into vanity overdrive. You can pick out the competitive focus in the following: "I think my opportunities for development are better than they were when we first started because I have more time to ask myself, 'What's the best way for me to do this? How can I do that better?'"

Sandy's underlying pattern was now driving her to seek results in a process designed to release herself from her compulsion to seek results!

The Three's spiritual path of *truthfulness* means being true to the moment, *being* instead of *doing*. When Sandy began to see and accept herself in the present she said, "Time out! I've worked 15-hour days as long as I can remember," and for the first time spent an entire weekend away from work and with her family.

> *You must accept yourself as you are, instead of as you would like to be, which means giving up self-deception and wishful thinking. As long as you regard yourself or any part of your experience as "the dream come true," you are involved in self-deception.* Chogyam Trungpa, *Cutting Through Spiritual Materialism*

SINGING IN OUR CHAINS

Oh as I was young and easy in the mercy of his means
Time held me green and dying
Though I sang in my chains like the sea.
   (Dylan Thomas, "Fern Hill")

Enneagram Fours represent our search for soul. This search can become so anguished, life is lived through a veil of pain. Dylan Thomas could *sing in his chains* because he also remembered being *green and carefree, famous among the barns / About the happy yard and singing* where *Time let me play and be / Golden in the mercy of his means.*

Fours, in contrast, tend to remember an anguished past and to focus on their longings for the future, which can keep them from appreciating the present.

Nicholas Cage captured this quality in an interview with Mirabella magazine*:* "I was the outsider, the weirdo, the kid who wasn't picked to go on the team." He said Jim Morrison had "never done a song that conveyed pure happiness. It was a warning to not stay on the dark side and be Angst Man."

While unenlightened Fours are attached to their pain, from the fixation of *dissatisfaction*, Fours often forge compassion from their empathy for others in a painful world. One of my Four clients recalled as a child having a "Feelings Club" in a tree house. "You were allowed to cry there and not be called on it."

I liken Fours at their best to the *bodhisattva*, who reject relief from reincarnation and return to help free others from suffering. The *boddhisattva's* choice, however, is voluntary and not a return engagement because of attachment to pain.

Satori for Fours is manifested in *equanimity*; seeing that all events are intrinsically neutral, that only desire grades things as "good" or "bad."

At their best Fours contribute to groups with their perspective from the outside, where they live, and often in innovative ways. But there's a time and a place for change, and always being dissatisfied with how things are becomes a set of chains.

With Fours the fixation of *dissatisfaction* arises from the passion of *envy*, often experienced as unhappiness with self and the ordinariness of one's life. Whenever we obsess on being special, driven to create something unique, we are experiencing the passion of the Four.

Even feeling sad or depressed can create a "special" identity. While any of us can be depressed, and seriously so, the angst of the Four is experienced as a deep, soulful sadness. In the same way each of us has pressed on an aching tooth to see if it still hurts, unawakened Fours press on their own pain. This quality brought us the unique expression of Vincent Van Gogh. But it also feeds attachment to pain.

A change in perspective for Fours can result from reviewing their past history, focusing on good things they've experienced, and noticing how often they've created their own dissatisfaction. The Buddhist way is to go even beyond that, to reach a level of enlightened equanimity, to relate to the world directly, without judgment, without involvement of an ego-strategy.

> *You only arrive at the other shore when you finally realize there is no other shore... we have arrived when we realize we were there all along.* Chogyam Trungpa, *Cutting Through Spiritual Materialism*

When we can "sing in our chains like the sea," we realize even the chains are illusory.

HOLDING THE SPADE IN OUR EMPTY HANDS

The brilliant British astrophysicist, Stephen Hawking, is an excellent exemplar of the Enneagram Five. Now 72 years old, he has suffered from Lou Gehrig's disease since his early twenties, when he was told he had only a few years to live. Someone else in his place might have fulfilled that prognosis, but in a way Hawking doesn't need his body.

Fives are extremely resourceful and the most independent of the nine Enneagram styles. Their self-sufficiency stems from a restriction of emotional needs—so no one becomes indispensable to them. They're often very bright and channel their profound feelings through intellect.

In Enneagram terms the Five's passion is *hoarding*, with a fixation on *detachment*—withdrawing from emotional connection. In *Transformation Through Insight* Claudio Naranjo suggests Fives' main characteristic is "non-involvement in relations, in life and even in ongoing experience... they do not look forward to contact with others as enriching, and therefore anticipate being depleted."

This explains the label of "hoarding" which may include hoarding of information, money, or possessions (my first husband was a Five who proudly wore a T-shirt that had been his father's in high school), but is most importantly a hoarding of Self.

The Five's path of transformation is highly representative of the shift in perspective required of us all: letting go of reliance on logic alone, realizing intuitively the world is not as we have known it to be. As the shift occurs we see how our attachment to knowing has led us to define ourselves through dualistic modes of thinking and kept us from intimacy—with others, with ourselves, and with the Infinite.

The *paramita* that parallels the Five's path is *generosity*, giving freely so energy flows outward. This is not "generosity" in the sense of giving things. In Enneagram theory it requires nonattachment, as described by Naranjo in one of his workshops

> ...*as in an open hand, more of an attitude of living in the present, allowing what comes naturally, a flow between self and others in which you receive more and give more.*

I have a Five friend who gave me an example of her *withdrawing* in a brunch at my house where all three couples had recently connected. It was near Valentine's Day, and my Two friend asked each couple to talk about how they fell in love. "I wanted to die," she said.

Since then, she's changed her work from an emphasis on building mental models toward close connection and affection with her clients. This happened naturally as she developed trust and intimacy with her husband. In the process she is rediscovering her whole Self.

> *However paradoxical it may seem, Zen insists that the spade must be held in your empty hands, and that it is not the water but the bridge that is flowing under your feet... the ordinary logical process of reasoning is powerless to give final satisfaction to our deepest spiritual needs.* D.T. Suzuki, *An Introduction to Zen Buddhism*

SWIMMING WITH THE DOLPHINS

As I approached a significant age milestone I longed to have a tattoo. I was changing in self-concept, defining myself outside others' expectations, and settled on a dolphin swimming around my left side—to symbolize awakening heart energy.

My friends were intrigued and I was on a bit of a high. Then I told my mother. Her response: "Why would you want to disfigure yourself?"

I felt like a child, completely devastated. And I know everyone who reads this has had similar experiences, coming up against the almost insurmountable authority of social conditioning and the wish to be accepted.

This dilemma is paramount for Enneagram Sixes. Their early experience was of powerlessness to predict where danger lay. "Who will punish me for being spontaneous? Who will criticize me for not doing what I was supposed to do?" And for some, "Where do I hide to keep myself safe?"

We all share these experiences to some degree, but for Sixes it becomes a passion, a constant fear like whistling in the dark: "I'm not afraid! I'm not afraid!" This ranges from internal churning over "What do I do here? What path do I take?" to a parody of the typical Woody Allen character. At the other extreme is counterphobic, reckless courage, but all these manifestations stem from deeply motivated fear.

Sixes' hypervigilance develops a highly developed set of antennae, bringing the gift of foresight as a way to counter fear: "If I can predict everything that can go wrong then I will be safe." But there is a paradox here. When we act as if we are powerless, in that very act we give our power away.

Furthermore, in this world we continually re-create—where others hold power over us—there is a desire to disempower the other. Thus the Sixes' fixation on *accusation*. Unawakened

Sixes seem to be in perpetual turmoil, aware of their own anxiety, shame, or anger—but pointing the finger outward: "If I'm powerless it must be somebody else's fault!"

When I told my mother about my tattoo I only wanted approval, and therefore her criticism was devastating. My first reaction was anger, and an accusation (to myself) of how "she always—in spite of her generally loving presence—could undermine my attempts to break the mold!"

Had I come from my center, from my own integrity, from my Dolphin heart, had I let go of my attachment to her approval, I would have been free of blame, perhaps touched by her own fear of change, or even admiring her for speaking her mind.

This is how I interpret the Buddhist perfection of *morality*: recognizing our own contribution to situations instead of playing victim. In Enneagram theory the *virtue* of the Six is *courage*, which is consistent with *morality*—releasing fear releases the need to blame. To let go of accusing others requires the courage to be with our own fear.

The space inside an empty vase is exactly the same as the space outside, separated only by the vase's wall. So our buddha nature is enclosed in the walls of our ordinary, conditioned identity. We are already there, where our hearts are, if only we cease to be deluded that there is any separation:

> *Happy, they leap out of the surface of waves...*
> *Curving, they draw curlicues and serifs with lashed tail and fin...*
> *Images of their delight outside, displaying my heart within...*
> *With power to wake me prisoned in my human speech they sign: 'I AM!'*
> (Stephen Spender, "Dolphins")

THE BEAUTY IN THE BEAST

In an ongoing e-mail correspondence with a Seven friend, I sent a quote from Sogyal Rinpoche's *The Tibetan Book of Living and Dying*:

> *Ask yourself, "Has my understanding of death and impermanence become so keen and so urgent that I am devoting every second to the pursuit of enlightenment?"*

"So really," I joked, anticipating his dread, "I sent this to you as a spiritually uplifting message."

His response: "Sure, that's easy for you to say. But we Sevens navigate the shoals of life by denial. This death stuff is a bit hard to deny." This same friend told me, when he lost his job, he was "depressed for about 20 minutes." Then he started listing all the benefits of this life change.

Charming, lively, playful, and curious, Sevens are characteristically buoyant and optimistic. Their fixation is *enthusiasm*, which is driven by the passion of *gluttony*. They want to experience everything and to do so with joy. But their determined cheerfulness is a coping strategy developed as children to blunt or cover up any pain. Because they've avoided pain all their lives, their pain threshold is low and they feel pain deeply. This only reinforces the desire to avoid it.

We can all identify with the urge to escape pain by doing something pleasurable. When my mother was 85 years old, she fell from a ladder, broke three ribs and a shoulder blade. Her lungs nearly collapsed because it hurt so much to breathe. What was her first reaction? To avoid the pain, even at the risk of death.

What was my first reaction when I feared she might die? "I think I'll go get some candy, buy a bottle of wine." Luckily I heard myself and held my feet to the fire of grief. As I did so, I wept over the pain of her potential loss and released the need to escape. I also dreamed about bereavement and about facing my own death. Staying with her was not a fun two weeks. But I came home feeling centered.

A Seven I once worked with was asked to tell his teammates how he thought his Enneagram coping strategy arose. He described how poor his family had been and how his schoolmates taunted him for being "from the wrong side of the tracks." But he hastened to gloss this over as a "minor aspect of a really great childhood."

Then a Six teammate described her warm relationship with her five siblings—in league against two alcoholic parents—and the terrible grief she felt when the sister she was closest to died of leukemia. Everyone in the group was touched by her emotional recall, but none of us was prepared for the reaction of the Seven.

He started with, "I'd like to say something here..." and then was completely wrenched with tears. He was finally able to say in a choked voice, "Such pain... such pain..." Of course he was feeling his own pain he had so casually denied.

Transformation for the Seven lies in recognizing gluttony as an ego-trap designed to escape from the reality of life—which holds both pain and pleasure. Paralleling this path among the Buddhist *paramita* on the path to *satori* is *renunciation*—seeking moderation or temperance.

But temperance only opens the door to further work. When we no longer seek escape through materialistic pleasures, we begin to dive beneath the surface, to stay with our fullest and deepest reality.

I once attended a Jungian workshop where we were asked to write about integrating our *shadow* (parts of ourselves we've buried because they don't fit our idealized self-image). I wrote a poem titled "Beauty and the Beast" where the image of "Beauty" is Anne Boleyn, who was beheaded because she refused to disown her child. I found myself describing the

"Beast" (the *shadow*) as "never satiated" and "longing with sad eyes—a tender Bigfoot." I imagined the integration of *shadow* as the "Beautiful Beast."

Because Sevens engage in positive reframing to a fault, I offer an invitation to awakening through a negative reframe: an excerpt from Paul Zimmer's poem, "Zimmer Resisting Temperance." It captures the zest and humor as well as the longing for depth and spirituality of Sevens:

> *Some people view life as food served*
> *By a psychopath. They do not trust it.*
> *But Zimmer expects always to be happy...*
>
> *Someday he may fall face down*
> *In the puke of his own buoyancy,*
> *But while the world and his body*
> *Are breaking down,*
> *Zimmer will hold his glass up.*

TAKE REFUGE IN THE COMMUNITY

"My years as a mercenary ended," said Ed, an Enneagram Eight, "when I was walking down a street with a woman, and a kid reached out and pushed her. He was with a bunch of other kids and they were just goofing off—it was basically harmless—but without thinking I struck out and Whop! hit him hard in the face.

"The woman with me didn't realize what had happened because we kept on walking, but I know I left that kid with some broken bones. I don't think I killed him, but that was the end of that life for me. I realized something in me was becoming damaged. I asked myself, 'Along the road I'm going, what can become of me? Who would I be?' Certainly no one I could live with."

The Eight's fixation on *power and control* stems from the passion of *excess*—an unexamined Eight wants it all and wants it NOW! They tend to be rougher, tougher people, more aggressive, more confrontive, more intent on winning. But as with all Enneagram styles this is only the outward manifestation of a life-long coping strategy: to protect their soft hearts by never showing vulnerability, as if the child inside who was never expressed continues to need constant protection.

Eights got the message as children they were on their own and had to grow up fast. I can usually reach this soft interior by asking them to think of rocking a baby in their arms and saying, "You never, ever had the experience that it was safe to let go like this, to trust in the shelter of your innocence, to simply be a baby."

This is why some Enneagram teachers express the path of awakening for Eights as a return to innocence—the ability to trust, to place oneself in the arms of the lover, the family, the community.

Unawakened Eights compensate for the injustice of not having had a real childhood by taking "justice" into their own hands, taking charge of things. Even the least self-aware Eights are typically protective of children, but in general need to develop their tender side. This can show up early on as tenderness in relationship with a lover or friend. As their level of trust grows, their compassion grows as well.

From a Buddhist perspective we could say *wisdom* is an Eight way to *satori*. But in Buddhism, wisdom and compassion are inseparably linked; thus true wisdom reflects a shift to more altruistic and benign modes of operating, a focus on service to the world. In Enneagram theory, as well, the enlightened Eight is one who reflects the highest qualities of the Two (whose path is loving-kindness). A Buddhist chant reminds us of three refuges on our path:

> *I take refuge in the Buddha (commitment to enlightenment), I take refuge in the Dharma (commitment to the teachings), I take refuge in the Sangha (commitment to the community of seekers)*

In community we can all put ourselves in others' shoes and allow our hearts to go out to the weak and strong alike, when we're no longer afraid to embrace our own vulnerabilities:

> *If I identify with any side of any position, my attachment to that side makes me see the opposite side in terms of an object, as "them"... which increases the psychic distance between people... put your own consciousness in a place where you are no longer attached to a polarized position... Until I was centered enough, till I was in that place in myself, I couldn't really know that place in other beings.* Ram Dass, *The Only Dance There Is*

An Eight found himself weeping during a tender conversation. He said, "I don't know what's happened to me. I used to be so tough, and now I 'leak' all the time!" We know what happened.

BREATHE IN, BREATHE OUT

In The Karate Kid, a teenaged boy who comes to his teacher's home to learn karate is at first given only menial tasks: "Wax these cars—wax on with right hand, off with left hand, breathe in, breathe out. Sand this deck—right hand in circle, left hand in circle, breathe in, breathe out. Paint fence—wrist up, wrist down, right hand, left hand. Paint house, side to side, right hand, left hand."

Finally, the boy explodes: "You're supposed to be teaching me, but for four days I've been busting my ass and I haven't learned a g.d. thing."

"You learn plenty," says the teacher, and as the boy storms off commands him to return and face him. "Look into my eyes—show me sand floor."

The boy reluctantly makes the circles with his right and then left hand and the teacher throws punches that are blocked by the boy's sweeping hands.

"Show me, wax on, wax off. Show me paint the fence. Show me paint the house."

And as the boy makes these deeply practiced and spontaneous movements, the teacher demonstrates how each has its place in karate. When this lesson is completed, without a word of explanation, the teacher bows.

This is in the Zen tradition of a student asking "What is the meaning of life?" and the Master hitting the student with a stick. Right. I didn't get it for a long time either.

Nor did I "get it" the first few days of an Enneagram workshop with Claudio Naranjo and Suzanne Stroke that focused on Enneagram transformation. I came expecting I would be *taught* the steps to transformation, have my questions answered, and overcome my "faults" as a Nine. "So why," I ranted to myself, "are they spending so much time on these meditation and relationship exercises, these visualizations? These have nothing to do with the Enneagram! When is he going to start the teaching?"

"Close your eyes," said Naranjo, "breathe in, breathe out, imagine a holy light shining down through the top of your head and filling your whole body with love. Now, open your eyes and look at your partner. Do not speak, breathe in, breathe out, and let this light shine through you to your partner. Do not respond when it is their turn to speak about their compulsions, do not judge, simply be present with your partner and with the light."

And so the workshop went on. We did "simple" exercises that deepened our understanding of how our habitual responses become engaged, our unconscious pay-offs for maintaining the status quo, how we stop ourselves from disclosing because we have an image to maintain or because we fear the discomfort it will bring, how we project our shortcomings onto others, especially in close relationships.

Operating from the Nine's fixation of *self-forgetting* we Nines too easily look for others to provide a structure, and through that structure discover what we *don't* want. I wanted to be *told* how to remember myself. I didn't know in the beginning I *was* remembering myself, These experiences were to *reflect myself to me* in the context of my Enneagram style.

In *Enneagram Spirituality*, Suzanne Zuercher describes the importance to our transformation of *active contemplation*—as opposed to passive surrender to the process. Active contemplation is similar in concept to Buddhist *mindfulness*, a posture of awareness, intention, and readiness throughout daily life:

- *Awareness*—of your Enneagram style and how it plays out uniquely for you. The passion of Nines is *indolence*, a kind of lassitude regarding our own agenda).

- *Intention*—commitment to your own "holy idea" or path to *satori*. For Nines it's the Buddhist perfection of *energy*, fully experiencing our wishes and emotions, acting on our own purpose, without distraction.

- *Readiness*—a holistic stance of invitation, of openness, as well as taking specific *actions* that shake things up, those that are most difficult for you, that invite your unknown and disowned parts to come forth; staying present with whatever shows up instead of avoiding or denying or projecting blame.

And this is just the beginning.

ABOUT THE AUTHOR

Mary Bast is a coach and coach mentor who works by phone with clients worldwide.

Author of *Somebody? Nobody? The Enneagram, Mindfulness and Life's Unfolding*; *Out of the Box: Coaching with the Enneagram*; *Out of the Box Self-Coaching Workbook,* and *Out of the Box Coaching Field Guide,* Mary is also a painter and writes poetry and memoir.

Out of the Box Coaching: http://www.breakoutofthebox.com
Coach Mentor: http://mentoringforcoaches.blogspot.com
Self-Coaching Tips: http://outoftheboxcoaching.blogspot.com
Fine Art: http://www.marybast.com
Poetry/Found Poetry: http://windingsheets.blogspot.com

Made in the USA
San Bernardino, CA
14 January 2017